MW01193321

Save Them From Secularism

Pre-Evangelism For Your Children

David de Bruyn

Save Them From Secularism: Pre-Evangelism for Your Children

Copyright © 2013 by David de Bruyn

All rights reserved. No part of this publication may be reproduced, stored in a retrieval system or transmitted in any form by any means, electronic, mechanical, photocopy, recording or otherwise, without prior permission of the publisher.

Cover art and design by Jonathan Cohen

Scripture taken from the New King James Version®. Copyright © 1982 by Thomas Nelson, Inc. Used by permission. All rights reserved.

Table of Contents

I

Secular Imaginations

This is not another book on how to preach the gospel to your children. It is a book about how to *prepare* them for the gospel. It's a book about shaping their attitude towards the gospel.

I assume, if you're reading this, that you want to see your child profess Christ and follow Him all the days of his or her life. I therefore take it for granted that you will be teaching the child the gospel, exposing him to biblical truth, and calling on her to repent and believe.

My concern in this book is why fewer and fewer children from ostensibly Christian homes are professing the gospel, and why only a fraction of those are continuing on as lifelong disciples.

Studies by Barna, for what they are worth, show that most children growing up in evangelical churches will abandon the faith. According to those reports, even though many of those who drop out of church are actively involved in church during their teen years, by their early twenties most have stopped participating actively in the Christian faith. In total, six out of ten twentysomethings dropped out of church and general Christian living. Worse, it's not just a temporary phase, but the trend seems to be continuing deeper into adulthood, even when those who have dropped out of church have children of their own.[1] In other words, such people, who grew up in evangelical churches, are well and truly denying the faith with their lives.

All kinds of reasons have been proposed for this phenomenon: the age-segregation of the church, shallow youth ministry, inconsistency of Christian adults, lack of spiritual leadership in the home, lack of serious discipleship in the local church, and proliferation of unwholesome media. Any or all of these may be contributing factors. However, it seems what is missing in these conversations is how a child's disposition towards Christianity is shaped long before he or she encounters the truths of the gospel, or the demands of discipleship.

Before the child is able to weigh the propositions that explain the gospel, or consider the validity of biblical teaching, he already has prejudices for or against the claims of Christ. He either has a disposition, a *sensibility* that Christianity is true and good and beautiful and ought to be embraced, or he does not. As he grows, this sense increases or decreases in either direction, and largely shapes how he interprets the facts of Christianity as they are placed before him.

---

1 .See http://www.barna.org/barna-update/article/16-teensnext-gen/147-most-twentysomethings-put-christianity-on-the-shelf-following-spiritually-active-teen-years

In other words, a child is no *tabula rasa* (blank slate). He arrives with a set of faculties that immediately begin to make sense of the world by interpreting the raw data of the world through an ever-growing 'grid' of interpretations, sensibilities and dispositions. No fact he encounters is understood on its own; it is understood through a network of other facts, feelings and desires. This includes facts such as *Jesus is the Son of God, Hell actually exists*, and *Jesus deserves your total allegiance and ultimate love*. How the person responds to those statements, both when he is five and twenty-five, is largely a result of this grid.

Another term for this grid is the *imagination*. How a person imagines reality in totality, how he pictures ultimate things that make sense of the raw data of his life, how he places value on things and orders them, is his imagination. This imagination can either be Christian or non-Christian. It can be religious or secular. And it is shaped long before the child can read or answer catechism questions.

J. Gresham Machen put it this way: "...[I]t would be a great mistake to suppose that all men are equally well prepared to receive the gospel. It is true that the decisive thing is the regenerative power of God. That can overcome all lack of preparation, and the absence of that makes even the best preparation useless. But as a matter of fact God usually exerts that power in connection with certain prior conditions of the human mind, and it should be ours to create, so far as we can, with the help of God, those favourable conditions for the reception of the gospel."[2]

It's my belief that many of the evangelical dropouts we witness today are abandoning the faith because they grew up with a fundamentally secular imagination, with a thin Christian overlay. Over time, or as a result of some life circumstance, the underlying grid pushes the person to re-evaluate his beliefs and align them more consistently with the grid. Since the grid is essentially one that views God as a weightless, if not non-existent concern, at some point the thoughtful person recognises that his Christian faith is a wrinkle in his worldview, an error in the program, an extraneous digit that does not belong. Consequently, he announces that he "no longer believes".

The question for Christian parents becomes, how is that grid shaped? How does one shape the imagination so that the child has a prejudice towards Christianity's truths, both before and long after he has embraced them? Parents need to think long and hard how to shape those prior conditions of the mind.

Understanding the Imagination

If we want our children to love and embrace the 'facts' of the gospel, we need to step back and think about how children gain their knowledge. In fact, we need to step back and think about knowledge itself.

We're surrounded by a scientistic (note: not merely *scientific*) culture that likes to see itself as interested in only 'objective facts'. For this kind of thinking, the keys to understanding the world are a good microscope, telescope, computer or any other instrument that can record *objective* facts about the world. If we collect enough of these objective facts from the sciences of physics, chemistry, geoscience, astronomy, genetics and the like, we will understand reality, it reasons. This is *real* knowledge, it boasts. None of those *subjective* values and personal judgements about religion, morality, ethics, beauty or truth are to be considered – those are mere preferences, you see. Those are not testable, verifiable or measurable in a laboratory, therefore they are simply statements of human opinion or desire, but do not represent reality. If we want to know reality, and understand ultimate questions such as who we are, how we got here, where we are going, what we are here for, we must turn to the 'objective' sciences. Knowing reality then, becomes an exercise in fact-collecting. Supposedly, collect enough of these autonomous, scientific facts, and you will know reality.

Most modern school curricula reflect this modernist thinking. Pick up the textbooks, listen in on the lessons, and you'll observe it. Reality, to them, is a collection of raw, uninterpreted facts, and therefore a child must collect as many of these as possible, as unrelated or eclectic as these facts might be. Math facts, history facts, geography facts, chemistry facts, biology facts, language facts, and social sciences facts (the most laughable of all) – if a child completes a good twelve years of this kind of fact-collecting, then he is 'educated'. Nothing unifies or binds all these facts, nor is a child supposed to weigh them for their goodness or beauty. He should just collect them, get the certificate, and get a job.

The problem with this whole endeavour is that is incredibly conceited, and blind to its own arrogance. This idea of the perfect objectivity of science, and the supposed unreliable subjectivity of art and faith, was a conceit of the Enlightenment. In truth, all 'facts' are known by subjects – us. We understand the *meaning* of the facts under consideration, the *value* of the facts we're seeing, only by connecting them with a much bigger grid of understanding. That grid is the imagination.

In other words, though objective reality exists outside of us, we only know that reality as perceiving subjects. We perceive that reality through a pre-existing grid which interprets the facts. The grid, or the imagination, determines how we will understand the raw data of the world that is given to us. If the grid is wrong, it will misconstrue what it sees 100% of the time. The telescope might be flawless, but that's not the point. Humans use those telescopes and decide what the data means.

Romans 1 makes this idea fairly clear. Once the grid of ultimate devotion to God was abandoned and replaced with a grid of idolatry, mankind became increasingly deceived in his perceptions of the world.

> because, although they knew God, they did not glorify Him as God, nor were thankful, but became futile in their thoughts, and their foolish hearts were darkened. Professing to be wise, they became fools (Ro 1:21-22).

Man's fact-collecting mission would now always arrive at the wrong conclusions, because his grid was now idolatrous.

Why all this discussion of knowledge and objectivity in a conversation about child evangelism? Because many Christian parents have embraced the modernist idea of collecting objective facts, when it comes to educating their children. Theirs is identical to a secularist's approach, except that to the list of algebra facts, economics facts and art facts, they add Bible facts. They believe that they must simply supplement the secular information with some Christian information, and all will turn out well. Years later, their children, now young adults, announce that they no longer believe what they were taught in Sunday School. What happened? Did the

Bible facts change in their content? Did the child discover that those facts were not objective?

What happened is that the child's *interpretation* of those Bible facts changed. His *feeling* towards the biblical data changed, which in turn, changed the *meaning*, the interpretation of those Bible facts, in his mind. And it changed because of what was going on behind the facts – in his imagination.

For Christians, the shaping of the imagination becomes particularly crucial, because not only do we want our children to interpret the raw sensory data of the world according to God's view of reality, we need them to understand many things that cannot be seen – God's attributes, grace, justice, nobility, holiness, judgement, to name just a few. They will only understand these ultimate unseen realities through the imagination – through the analogies that explain the unseen with the seen. If their imaginations are filled with incorrect analogies, they will misconstrue and misunderstand unseen realities that are critical to the gospel and the Christian life. Worse, they will respond to those realities wrongly, treating them differently to what they are.

A parent's role is far more than entering facts into the child's CPU, as if a human soul could be compared to a computer. A parent has twenty years or so to shape a child's picture of reality. He or she is a crucial part of putting together a child's internal mental map, using all kinds of analogies. As we build these analogies, we are not only shaping a child's grid, we are teaching him how he ought to *feel* about the facts he will encounter. Before the child's vocabulary has even filled out, we are providing him with a sense of proportion: *this* is like *that*, and *deserves* this kind of response. I say again, many parents think the goal of training is the imparting of cognitive knowledge. However, if you would like your child to rightly interpret the knowledge he encounters, you must shape his imagination through analogous knowledge.

How do we build analogous knowledge? There are several ways that emerge from Scriptural example and from the world that God has created. The next chapters will examine them.

II

Parental Piety

The first and greatest commandment is followed by a commandment to teach children to do the same (Deut 6:4-9). Our goal as Christian parents should be nothing less than to help shape our children so that they will, by grace, become ardent lovers of God. We have said this happens not merely by telling our children to love God, but by shaping the child's imagination.

Probably one of the first analogies the child's imagination receives is the analogy of his parents' piety. This provides him with a picture of what it is like to be in a relationship with God.

Before a child knows anything about justification, penal substitution, or the nature of God, he knows what a relationship with God is like. Or at least, he knows what his believing parents express it to be like. The religious imagination of child is shaped by being exposed to his parents' piety, and it is their example that gives him his first introduction to *how* God is to be loved, and if God *ought* to be loved.

This is probably why right after telling Israel that they are to love Him with all the heart, soul and might, God tells them that these words about loving God ultimately "which I command you today shall be in your heart." That is, these words are to be internalised and understood and practised by the parents themselves first. Following that, verse 7 kicks in.

> "You shall teach them diligently to your children, and shall talk of them when you sit in your house, when you walk by the way, when you lie down, and when you rise up."

Certainly, this teaching will take the form of direct instruction. However, our concern in this book is how the non-discursive, non-cognitive faculty of knowing is shaped. Certainly then, part of the teaching is the fleshed-out example of love for God seen in the parents.

Loving God ultimately can be thought of as ultimate dependence, ultimate devotion and ultimate delight. When we love God ultimately, we regard Him as ultimately reliable, ultimately valuable, and ultimately desirable. We do not trust, commit to, or rejoice in anything besides God as an end. All else are means: He alone is the end.

In a family, this kind of love for God is seen in very tangible ways. When in the middle of a health or financial or emotional crisis, Dad says to the family, "We can be very thankful for what God has given us. Let's turn to Him now in prayer, and ask Him for grace", that lesson speaks to little hearts in powerful ways. Gratitude and contentment say more than 100 sermons. When Dad says, "We've barely got petrol in the tank, but we know God wants us to worship Him. We'll trust that God will enable what He commands." And do you know what God loves to do when those little eyes are watching that act of ultimate dependence? Provide. Supply. Protect.

When the child is groaning about a sore throat on Monday morning, and Dad says, "Get out of that bed, and get ready, you *are* going to school!" he is teaching the importance of education. But when the child has the same groans about a sore throat on Sunday morning, and Dad says, "Well, just take it easy and rest this morning," he has taught something else. He has taught that education takes priority over worship. He has taught that our devotion to education ought to exceed our devotion to God.

When Mom will drive from this side of the city for swimming to that side of the city for tennis or ballet, to the other side for extra maths, and back again for soccer, and finally home, racking up a good 100 kilometres in the process, the child might learn that Mom and Dad like him to have activities. But when they say, "We can't go to the Wednesday Evening service, it's too much driving, and petrol is getting more expensive", he learns about priorities. Petrol costs and driving time aren't an issue if it is extra-murals or education, but very high hurdles if it is church. He has just learnt *how* committed one should be to God, and it is not an ultimate commitment.

Children know what we love. They see it when our eyes sparkle when we talk about what delights us. They see how we anticipate the things we really love. They see how we reminisce over the things we love. And they see how we connect those things to God, if we do. They see what our attitude is towards the things of God.

If Dad's sighing heavily as everyone gets in the car on Sunday, but he's cheerfully buoyant before the start of a rugby game on TV, he communicates which brings more joy. If Mom is humming away while she copies photos to Facebook and makes scrap-book albums, but looks like she's eaten lemons during the singing of hymns, she communicates what brings her joy.

And make no mistake, those little eyes are on you in corporate worship – do you enjoy and understand those hymns, or do you just mouth them? Do you love God's Word and read it with hunger? Do you communicate your relish for the Word before and after? They notice when you're soaking in the Word, and they notice when you're looking at your watch. And later on, they might remember that you don't do that during a movie.

Before we *tell* them so, we *show* our children what we think is reliable, valuable and desirable. God says there is only One who deserves that kind of love. That should be the day-in, day-out message of our homes.

III

Family Roles

How a child imagines ultimate reality is powerfully shaped by his parents. How his parents live out their faith provides the child with an ongoing example of what a relationship with God is like, what loving God looks like, and why it *ought* to be chosen over secularism, materialism, or practical atheism.

However, the family unit is far more than a set of exemplars of piety. The family is also a collection of living symbols. The home is an extended role-play, and an ongoing metaphor. Each member plays a role, and with that role comes corresponding relationships. These roles have analogues in ultimate reality. Husband, wife, father, mother, and child take on particular roles that illustrate intangible moral realities.

In the home, the children observe this role-play for more or less twenty years. Though the mundaneness of life seems to hide it, family roles are teaching the children about ultimate reality. They teach about authority, and how it should be exercised. They teach about obedience and disobedience, the reasons for obedience, and the consequences of obedience and disobedience. They teach about love: that there are different degrees of love, and different kinds of love. They teach about gospel realities: sin, righteousness, sacrifice, service, grace and mercy, forgiveness, and trust.

Before your child has pronounced the word "God", he has an idea of authority. Before your child has ever heard about Hell, she has learned whether or not selfishness has negative consequences. Before your children have ever memorised John 3:16, they have observed some kind of love in the home.

Two areas are of particular importance to the religious imagination: the portrayal of the loving authority of God which inspires and expects both obedience and reverence, and the portrayal of the sovereign grace that both nourishes and cherishes the beloved. In other words, children need a vision of God's greatness and His goodness, His transcendence and His immanence.

Fathers (and mothers) aim to be pictures of a God who rules justly and fairly, but regards rebellion as a deep perverseness that must not be allowed to continue unchecked. The kind of obedience God expects from us (immediate, cheerful, wholehearted) is the kind fathers aim to inspire and expect. Likewise, the father in particular wants to be a picture of a God to be revered, honoured and esteemed and who regards irreverence with the same deep concern. The kind of respect which a child will show to his Ultimate Authority must at least begin in seed-form with his honouring of his parents (and I might add, his grandparents, pastors, teachers, policemen, governors, and so forth). And, we hasten to add, there is a kind of deportment from those authorities that inspires reverence (Tis 2:2-3). Ideally, children will see a model of submission and reverence when they behold their mother in her role as a wife (Eph 5:22, 33).

Mothers (and fathers) aim to be pictures of a God who seeks to sacrificially meet the needs of those He loves, and regards them as precious. This nourishing and cherishing is to be true of husbands towards wives, and of fathers and mothers toward children (Eph 5:29, 1 Thes 2:7, 11). For that matter, biblical masculinity and femininity are more than biological realities or practical arrangements, they are shadows of unseen truths. When rightly lived out, children see copies of the true (Heb 9:24).

Recently, good books have been written on how Christian parents are to go beyond dealing with mere outward behaviour, and aim instead for the child's beliefs and heart desires.[3] These books commendably exhort child-training to push a child to the gospel itself. Let us push further. Our goal is more than acquaintance with the facts of the gospel. It is for our children to imagine all the realities connected to the gospel properly, and to feel rightly towards those realities.

---

3   For example, *Shepherding a Child's Heart,* by Tedd Tripp, (Wapwallopen, PA: Shepherd Press, 1995).

If we do our best to be obedient to the biblical roles in the power of the Holy Spirit, we fill our homes with something quite extraordinary: an ongoing, albeit imperfect, picture of the Creator who rules, but who also redeems and restores. Once again, children will learn not just that they are commanded to love God, but that loving God is good. They learn, if a relationship with Christ is like their parents' marriage, then loving God is *desirable*. If God cares for them like their mother, then it is *safe* trusting God wholeheartedly. If God is as just and strict as their parents, then they *need* their sins forgiven. If God is a Father like their father, then they *owe* Him deep and joyful respect. One of the most important ways we shape our children's imaginations is by seeking to put off worldly patterns of marriage and family, and putting on patterns we find in Scriptures such as Ephesians 5:22-6:4, Colossians 3:18-21, and 1 Peter 3:1-7.

When preachers make statements about Satan's intentions to destroy the family, they are probably not far off the mark. To ruin the analogy is to ruin the child's chance of picturing ultimate reality properly, robbing him of a right view of the gospel's realities. To give a fairly appropriate portrayal of who God is, what He is like, what obstructs knowing Him, and how we come to know Him is to provide, in the words of J. Gresham Machen, favourable conditions for the reception of the gospel, which the Spirit may be pleased to use.

IV

Routines

Another powerful shaping influence on a child's imagination is a family's routines. Deuteronomy 6:7 says,

> "You shall teach them diligently to your children, and shall talk of them when you sit in your house, when you walk by the way, when you lie down, and when you rise up."

Here God tells Israel that their teaching and talking about loving God (vv4-5) must take place when they sit in the house, and when they walk by the way, when they lie down and when they rise up. On one level, God is simply pointing out how this discipling relationship must take place formally and informally, indoors and outdoors. But in another way, God's words suggest the rhythm and routine of life. *When you sit in the house* is the time of day when you are at home; *when you walk by the way* is the time of day when you go out. *When you lie down* is the time of day when you sleep; *when you rise up* is the time of day when you wake from your sleep. Here is a suggestion of a cycle of events, a routine, a rhythm of life – getting up in the morning, going out, coming back, lying down to sleep. Not only are you to teach about loving God routinely, but *your routine itself* communicates something. Your daily, weekly, monthly, and even yearly routine teaches your family about ultimate dependence, ultimate devotion, and ultimate love.

For the Israelite, his daily routine involved reciting the Shema in the morning and in the evening. When he ate his meals, his restricted diet reminded him to put a difference between the holy and the common and he thought on God. When he worked the land, there were laws regarding the animals, laws regarding sowing, tilling and reaping, which caused him to think on God. If he went to transact business, there were laws about money and equity. When he went home, there were laws about ritual cleanness. Once a week, he was to cease work, for God's sake.

And if he was anywhere near the Tabernacle, or later, the Temple, he would have seen a routine: a burnt offering twice daily, and a meal offering twice daily – one in the morning, and one in the evening – when the day's activity began and when it ceased. There would have been a sacrifice every Sabbath, and a sacrifice at the beginning of each month. There were sacrifices at the special feasts of Passover, Pentecost, Day of Atonement, and Tabernacles. He was to go to the Tabernacle or Temple three times a year.

What did this routine communicate to him? God is at the centre of life. God is the ultimate reality. God is the One we love ultimately, because He is ultimate reality.

This is the opposite of secularism which tries to sideline God to the margins of life, relegating Him to a once-a-week appearance. Secularism has a daily routine in which God is essentially invisible, and practically irrelevant. Secularism has a routine which suggests that God does not matter. Many children grow up in Christian homes that are *practically* secular. The routine reflects nothing of the idea that God is that family's ultimate love.

A New Testament Christian does not exist under the same code as the Israelite. Jesus told us to abide in Him as He abides in us. The word *abide* simply means to dwell, to live. We are to live in Him: live in His presence continually. When His words abide in us, and we are living before Him and in light of Him, then our routines ought to have Him as the ultimate reality behind all we do. These routines either have God present when you lie down, rise up, sit in the house or walk by the way or they do not.

Consider your home. How does each day typically begin? Is there anything of God in it? Does the day start with some kind of reading of the Word and prayer? Is there some equivalent of the morning sacrifice?

What is the habit around mealtimes, particularly dinnertime? Who is honoured for providing – which is, after all, why Dad was out all day – working hard so that God would be pleased to bless the home with provision. What is discussed at the table?

What kind of music routinely plays in the background? What sort of movies or TV programmes routinely play on the screen? Is the tenor of life one of distraction, or one of reflection?

How does the day end? Is there anything of God in it? Is there perhaps some family worship, some thanksgiving prayers before bedtime, or some music played which honours God? Is there some equivalent of the evening sacrifice?

When the days of rest come around, what is the routine then? Critically, what are the weekly habits of the family when the local church meets? Too many parents miss the fact that regular worship teaches those little hearts through the routine itself. Frequently I have heard adult Christians reflect on their childhood growing up in a Christian home, and saying that 'we didn't miss a service'. When an adult says that, he is not typically remembering the preaching or even the other acts of corporate worship. He is remembering a rhythm of life that demonstrated God's centrality to that family.

What is repeated over and over again is learnt, memorised, internalised, and usually, prioritised. The habits of your home become a kind of rhythm that your children learn to get in step with. Routines say, *this is important. This is necessary. This is essential.* Routines are a picture of what the cycles of life revolve around.

If we want our children to believe that the most important thing in life is a reconciled relationship with God, then we need to think about our rising up, going out, coming in, and lying down.

V

Rituals

We have considered how the parents' piety, roles in the home and routines are critical to shaping the child's religious imagination. We now consider a fourth powerful shaping force. Deuteronomy 6:8-9 says,

> You shall bind them as a sign on your
> hand, and they shall be as frontlets
> between your eyes. You shall write
> them on the doorposts of your house
> and on your gates.

It is possible that Moses wanted Israel to do something physical, such as writing out some Scripture, since people did not have a copy of the Law for themselves. But more than likely, God was saying through Moses that Israel was to fill their homes with things that served as signs and reminders of God as the ultimate reality. The Israelite home was to teach and instruct love for God not only by the piety of the parents, the godly roles, the manners, the God-centred routine, but also by ritual.

Evangelical Christians hear the word *ritual*, and typically respond with nervous suspicion. For those who prize genuine conversion and piety, ritual has connotations of dead religion, empty ceremony or even hypocrisy.

What is a ceremony or a ritual? It is an event which carries special meaning, performed on a special occasion. Weddings are rituals, ceremonies done on special occasions. All that we do at that ceremony has meaning: the way the bride and groom are dressed, what music is played, what is said, and the use of symbolic rings. The same is true of funerals, birthdays, graduations and inaugurations.

If you read the book of Leviticus, you will find that the worship and service of God in the Tabernacle, and later in the Temple, contained elaborate ceremony. The Levites followed God's prescriptions for the various rituals of cleansing and sacrifice to the letter. The Israelite's life was filled with laws, rituals and ceremonies, prescribed and designed by God. Here and there, God explained what the teaching purpose was of these rituals and ceremonies:

> "that you may distinguish between
> holy and unholy, and between unclean
> and clean." (Leviticus 10:10)

God filled the life of Israel with ceremonies that helped the Israelite to see the difference between worship and selfishness, between a life lived only for things under the sun, and a life lived with a perspective of things above the sun. To put it in modern language, God was rescuing the Israelite from practical atheism, from what we would call practical secularism. By clothing life in all kinds of symbols, God was frequently reminding and teaching that He was the ultimate reality.

Further, God knew that ceremony and ritual are some of the most memorable tools for teaching children.

> And you shall observe this thing as an ordinance for you and your sons forever. It will come to pass when you come to the land which the LORD will give you, just as He promised, that you shall keep this service. And it shall be, when your children say to you, 'What do you mean by this service?' "that you shall say, 'It is the Passover sacrifice of the LORD, who passed over the houses of the children of Israel in Egypt when He struck the Egyptians and delivered our households.' (Exodus 12:24-27)

Notice that God predicts that the ceremony will provoke a question from the child. That's the idea. Any well-planned ceremony has all kinds of symbols and procedures and manners which have meaning. It's the joy of children to observe and wonder, and the joy of parents to explain.

Inevitably, someone will say, "All that ritual belonged to the Old Testament. The New Testament is free of ceremony and form and ritual." Not true. What is baptism, but a ceremony, a ritual, in which we use a symbol to convey a deep, transcendent meaning? What is the Lord's Supper except a ritual, a ceremony, in which we use various symbols to convey special meaning? In fact, every Sunday worship service is a ceremony, in which we read the Scriptures, pray the Scriptures, sing the Scriptures and preach the Scriptures. Properly done, this ceremony will deeply shape the imaginations of children who have yet to grasp the realities of the gospel.

God is not against ceremony or ritual. He is against ceremony and ritual that points only to itself. He is against ceremony with evaporated meaning, performed by loveless, disobedient hearts. He is against ceremony which is unbiblical or promotes a false gospel. He is against additions or subtractions from prescribed worship.

Which Rituals?

Some Christians have taken in a kind of neo-Platonism without knowing it. This taught that the body is evil (or at least inferior and irrelevant) and the spirit is good. Consequently, under the spell of these ideas, physical matters such as eating, drinking, smelling, tasting, and touching are seen as unspiritual and carnal or inferior. Instead, the *really* spiritual person focuses on acts like prayer and inner meditation. If someone thinks like a neo-Platonist, he will frown on the idea of ceremony. Ceremonies often involve sights, smells, sounds and even tastes.

Does this antipathy towards ceremony represent true spirituality? Consider, when God wants to remind us of the death of Jesus Christ, what does He have us do? We remember the Lord's death by eating and drinking in a ceremony that involves very physical, tangible elements. When we want to show that we are disciples of Christ, what do we do? We are immersed in water in a physical, tangible ceremony that depicts the truth. When we come together to worship, we sing psalms, hymns and spiritual songs, and that very audible music rings in our ears as we do so. God is not against the use of food, drink, sensation, or music to teach and to instruct.

For the shaping of the religious imagination, ceremony or ritual is vivid and memorable. It pictures ultimate and invisible realities. When it is explained, it teaches and instructs and shapes the heart in powerful ways.

For our purposes, the application is to Christian parents. What kind of rituals or ceremonies ought our children to view and, in some cases, participate in, to provide analogies of ultimate reality?

First of all, there is the ceremony of gathering with God's people for corporate worship, which families attend. In the Old Testament, the Bible makes a point of saying that when Israel gathered corporately, "Now all Judah, with their little ones, their wives, and their children, stood before the LORD."(2 Chr 20:13) Corporate worship is a ceremony and ritual that the family should prepare for and look to and honour. I am strongly in favour of children being present in our worship services, so that they can view the very rituals that will provoke their questions and fire their imaginations. (Not sure what Moses would have made of "Children's Passover".)

Even if a child does not understand all the elements in worship, he is being shaped. The Bible anticipated, and even desired, a child's puzzlement and consequent curiosity with corporate worship. The resulting questions are an enormous opportunity for teaching.

The ceremony, for a conservative Protestant like me, is not elaborate. It is reading the Word, singing the Word, praying the Word and preaching the Word. However, the wonder for the child comes in how these elements are handled. *How* do the men pray corporately in addressing God? *How* do the people sing – what sort of songs, what kinds of emotions and responses do these adults endorse as fitting in responding to the invisible God? What *kinds* of emotions do they seek to evoke in response to

God? *How* does the preacher proclaim the message of God to man? If you are fortunate, your children get to observe ordinate worship. That is, they see responses and proclamations of God that correspond to who He is in Scripture. This powerfully shapes the way they imagine God to be, long before they have embraced the gospel itself. If they imagine God to be a therapist, a boyfriend, a grandfather, a rock star – because of the kinds of songs and prayers offered in corporate worship – then that will shape their view of what the gospel is.

Beyond what is publicly prayed, preached or sung, the parents' attitude towards this ceremony speaks volumes. It paints a picture in itself. If corporate worship is regarded very highly, and set apart as unique, it enables our children to distinguish between the holy and the common. They recognise God is holy, majestic and to be loved ultimately.

Let's say I didn't believe that. Let's say I wanted to communicate to my child that Sunday worship was ordinary, that Sunday worship was commonplace, or that there was nothing transcendent or majestic happening. How might I communicate that to my child? If I wanted him to think that Sunday worship was no different to activities performed on Monday or Thursday or Friday, then one way to achieve that would be to dress him like any other day. If the ceremony of Sunday worship is as ordinary as any other day, then I would want to make sure the child feels that way.

And I'd make sure I dress that same way. But if I wanted him to think that the Lord's Day is unique, and that worship is something sacred, and not common, I would use the very physical, tangible thing called clothing to help communicate that message. Comes the objection: "Sounds like legalism. God looks at the heart, you know!" Yes, but the physical affects the spiritual. If you want your child to feel inside that the event is casual, then dress him that way on the outside.

We are thankful that the Reformation dealt with the false sacred/secular distinctions. But instead of consecrating all of life to God, some have taken that to mean that worship should seem as ordinary and mundane as any other activity. Their efforts do not elevate normal life to a state of consecration; instead, they debase everything. Instead of a deep sense of reality permeating worship, they end up with a profound sense of mundaneness. Instead of filling the Christian church with sincerity, they fill it with what is common. Life does not become elevated and consecrated; worship becomes predictable, everyday and ordinary. Awe and reverence is lost, and the small consolation is that "we're all so real about it."

When we are about to worship, we need to help our children to understand that we're going to do something important, and joyful and serious. That means we have to sit quietly, and pay attention. That's what we would tell them if we were in the Supreme Court, or if we were at a funeral, or at a military memorial. If we want the child to think lightly of it, then we should let them act as they would at a MacDonald's.

What about what we do before worship? If we want to communicate how special this day is, we begin preparing beforehand. We get things ready on Saturday night, because not only do we want to avoid the tension that comes from rushing on Sunday morning, but we want to communicate, "tomorrow is the *Lord's* Day." We get ready in advance.

After worship, we can use the Sunday dinner table to discuss what we saw of God in corporate worship that day. If, after church is over, all that happens is that the TV goes on, or the PlayStation comes out, the message is, "Well, we got that out of the way." But if we talk of the Word that afternoon, we communicate that we have just worshipped God with His people, and it has affected us. He is our ultimate devotion. How we use the rest of the day communicates much, particularly if we persist in calling it the Lord's Day, and not merely the Lord's *morning*.

In small and great ways, Sunday worship is shaping the religious imaginations of our children. What we do before and after corporate worship, how we worship, how we approach it, how we sit, how we sing, how we talk in the car on the way there and on the way home – all of this tells a child how he should imagine God.

A second ceremony we need to build into our lives is family worship. Family worship does not need to be elaborate. It needs to be sincere and thoughtful. Family worship is a time, ideally daily, but realistically several times a week, when the whole family gathers, and the father leads by reading the Word, explaining it, helping the family to understand it and apply it, and then to pray it – to respond to God in prayer, and even in song. Another ritual or ceremony that can partner with family worship is the dinner table. In Scripture, the table is the place of fellowship, the place of honouring those you love, the place of sacrifice and service, and the place of instruction. Isn't it interesting how often God instructs us and teaches us love for Himself over a meal?

The dinner table ought to be a ceremony we have every day. We open it with prayer. We eat together. We speak to each other of the day, of its blessings, of its challenges, of its lessons. We laugh together, learn together and enjoy each other. The table is a useful place for the father, if he's present, to relate life to God, to speak of His works, and His ways. When the dinner table is an event which is beautiful and memorable, it is one of the strongest rituals that will instil the love of God into a family's heart.

But what is fast replacing the dinner table is the TV tray and the coffee table. The television is the only speaker at meal times, while everyone silently munches away, glaring at the box. Parents, reclaim the dinner table. Reclaim a time for family worship.

A third kind of ceremony or ritual or tradition can be those you build around significant Christian holidays. Yes, the Christian is not commanded to celebrate Christmas or Good Friday or Ascension Day, but what opportunities the Christian holidays present!

Whatever your convictions about the celebration of Christmas or Easter, you should consider using those days as opportunities to build your own ceremonies in the home that will teach the truths represented by those days. Remember, God has given you the pattern in Scripture. We understand ultimate reality through symbols, and if we can taste, touch, smell, see and hear those symbols, they are all the more memorable.

In your home, what symbolic actions will honour our Saviour's Resurrection, and mark that day with significance? On Christmas, what do you do that celebrates the Incarnation of Jesus Christ? What do your ceremonies at home on Good Friday, or Passover, or Resurrection Sunday, communicate? Just another day? A day for more food? A day for self-indulgence? A day to see extended family? Or can we memorably symbolize ultimate truths on these days so that loving God is again on the doorposts of our houses and on our gates? [4]

---

4   For helpful suggestions, see Noel Piper, *Treasuring God in Our*

A fourth kind of ceremony would be the kind you develop as a family to mark special days or events that illustrate or teach God as the ultimate reality. *Raising A Modern-Day Knight*[5] is a book that contains some helpful suggestions for returning ceremony into the life of a growing young man, with Christ at the centre: ceremonies for birthdays, for adolescence, for graduation, for pledges of purity, for engagement, and so forth.

Don't dismiss the whole idea of ceremony, and turn all of life into a bland grey nothingness. If God built ritual and ceremony into Old Testament Israel's life, if He continued it with New Testament believers in baptism and the Lord's Supper and New Testament worship, we have all the precedent we need for family rituals and ceremonies which inscribe the love of God on the doorposts and gates of our homes. We need these signs and symbols which teach truth vividly, powerfully, and unforgettably.

The difficulty is that meaningful ceremonies take work. It takes great effort to have a worship service with beauty and unity and meaning. It takes ongoing diligence to have family devotions that are thoughtful and regular. It takes work to plan traditions and activities associated with biblical events. Ceremonies are costly, when they're done well. But when they are memorable and beautiful,

Traditions (Wheaton, IL: Crossway, 2007).

5   Authored by Robert Lewis (Carol Stream, IL: Tyndale House, 2007).

they become powerful tools for the shaping of the religious imaginations of our children.

One other form of ritual deserves its own chapter: the everyday rituals we call *manners*.

VI

Manners

Just about everyone has some story about the rudeness of children today. A tantrumming monster in a restaurant whose parents seem like royal attendants trying to assuage the wrath of a child prince or princess, insolent children who cannot so much as greet adults (let alone stand in their presence or offer them their seats), demanding brats that announce their dislikes and contempt in any situation, however humiliating to the parents, out-of-control school classrooms, vandal-like behaviour in other people's homes – these have become commonplace.

We should have expected it. As secularism grips the imaginations of people, we should expect to see manners in decline, or disappearing altogether. Manners come from a supernaturalistic worldview, not a secular one. And as secularism spreads, manners have less and less place. Consider three very non-secular functions of manners.

First, manners distinguish station, rank, office, status, age, and gender. Manners treat ladies as ladies, adults as adults, the elderly as elderly, magistrates as magistrates and so forth. Manners declare that people are more than advanced blobs of protoplasm, or trousered apes. We may be spiritually equal, and equal before the law, but our differing vocations, ages, and experiences call for different responses. As Peter put it, "Honour all *people*. Love the brotherhood. Fear God. Honour the king." (1 Peter 2:17) Paul affirms this: "Render therefore to all their due: taxes to whom taxes *are due*, customs to whom customs, fear to whom fear, honour to whom honour." (Romans 13:7) Secularism seeks to flatten out these distinctions, explaining them only in terms of societal function. A supernaturalistic worldview sees these differences reflecting God's design, and to honour them is to acknowledge Him.

Second, manners clothe life with spiritual meaning. They distinguish us from mere animals and demonstrate the transcendent nature of our existence. Manners turn meals into something more than sustenance, sex into more than mating, clothing into something more than covering, speech into more than advanced grunting. Manners clothe the merely material in etiquette and ceremony. We distance ourselves from brute beasts with table manners, modest clothing, respect for property, chivalry, waiting our turn, and so on. We clothe our mere physical appetites with a certain amount of decorum, transforming the very meaning of those acts into something more than mere survival and procreation.

Third, by making these distinctions, and filling person, place and thing with spiritual meaning, we are making value judgements. Christians believe there is a transcendent order, which filters down into a scale of values: some things or people *deserve* a certain kind of treatment. Some people and things *ought* to be respected. Some gestures or habits *are* offensive. Some things *are* obscene. Manners apportion certain moods, attitudes, and responses as fitting, appropriate, or ordinate to the respective person, place or thing. To say that something or someone deserves a particular mood or affection is to believe that the true, the good, and the beautiful are realities.

A child without manners begins to lose a sense of meaning. Without the knowledge that age, rank, office, station represent real differences in reality, he learns to collapse all distinctions. All things and people are alike. Their only distinctions are their relative importance to meeting his own needs.

Soon, a sense of transcendence disappears, and is replaced with a mere sense of arbitrary rule-keeping for one's own advancement. It is bad enough that he is told repeatedly that he is nothing more than an evolved ape, he is also told that manners are mere arbitrary conventions. His immaturity delights in flouting conventions anyway, but when his own authorities tell him (or show him) that manners are mere puffery, he will scorn them with self-confident relish. What manners he retains will be mere niceties to ingratiate himself with those he wishes to use.

Finally, all possibility of ordinate affections towards God is lost. All sense of appropriate gesture and response has gone; his only standard for judging appropriateness is how familiar or good it feels to him. He was born an idolater, but now he will be nothing else, for he will decide in advance how he wants to feel towards God. He will set up a god in his own image, worship it with emotions and gestures that make him feel comfortable, and congratulate himself for his piety.

For these reasons, manners are indispensable for inculcating a Christian imagination upon our children. They need to know that life is a symbol for ultimate realities, that our physical existence is by no means the extent of our existence, and that there are such things as ordinate and inordinate affections: towards God, the world, and self.

God wanted Hebrew parents to instil manners in their children, knowing that these very manners would lead to the fear of the Lord. Consider these Scriptures:

> Honour your father and your mother, that your days may be long upon the land which the LORD your God is giving you. (Exodus 20:12)

Every one of you shall revere his mother and his father, and keep My Sabbaths: I *am* the LORD your God. (Leviticus 19:3)

Rise in the presence of the aged, show respect for the elderly and revere your God. I am the LORD. (Leviticus 19:32)

The LORD will bring a nation against you from afar, from the end of the earth, as swift as the eagle flies, a nation whose language you will not understand, a nation of fierce countenance, which does not respect the elderly nor show favour to the young. (Deuteronomy 28:49-50)

The eye that mocks his father, And scorns obedience to his mother, The ravens of the valley will pick it out, And the young eagles will eat it. (Proverbs 30:17)

Not only so, but there were appropriate forms of dress, appropriate ways to eat, appropriate ways to treat your neighbour's property. In some ways, the clean and unclean distinctions were helping the Israelite imagination come to grips with *appropriateness*, how physical matters could represent spiritual truths, and how all things were to be ordered by God's Word.

New Testament Manners

Children, obey your parents in the Lord, for this is right. [2]"Honour your father and mother," which is the first commandment with promise: "that it may be well with you and you may live long on the earth." (Ephesians 6:1-3)

Children are here told not only to obey their parents, but to *honour* them. To "honour" father and mother is to do more than submit to their commands. It is to demonstrate in action and attitude that they occupy a place of sufficient weight in your life that you accord them a place of special treatment. Respectful titles, respectful tones of address, expressions of gratitude, cheerful submission, responses to commands will all help flesh out the idea of *honour*. All along, parents should be helping children to understand that this will help them understand what it is to fear God, to understand reverence and respect before God. After all, if you are rude before men whom you have seen, how can you be respectful before the God whom you have not seen?

By filling a child's life with manners, parents are not trying to teach their children to master some snooty badge of refinement. They are shaping the child's imagination to understand ordinate affection.

Parents should give attention to teaching cheerful greeting of adults, use of respectful titles and respectful tones of voice, expressions of gratitude, use of courteous words, polite table manners, politeness as a houseguest or as a host, respect for property, respect for a country's flag, neatness, chivalrous treatment of the opposite sex and of the elderly or infirm, and a host of other ways of expressing appropriate love and respect for one's neighbour.

If we do this for no other reason than to have children that are complimented for their manners, we are not doing much for their imaginations. But if we are helping our children to think about meaning, occasion, rank, state, and appropriate responses to God and man, we are giving them a biblical worldview.

VII

Art

When it comes to shaping a child's imagination – that part of him that will make sense of ultimate reality – little is more crucial than the arts. Music, poetry, literature, the plastic arts and theatre reach the imagination directly and shape it profoundly.

Unfortunately, many Christian parents have a concept of the arts that is profoundly secular. First, the arts are viewed primarily as entertainment, or as forms of distraction. Music is what you listen to 'to unwind', movies are a way to 'veg out', and books are forms of pleasant distraction. With this view, the most some Christian parents will do is to ensure that the forms of distraction do not contain nudity, profanity or excessive violence.

Second, the arts are seen as badges of refinement. Playing an instrument, reading the classics, and reciting good poetry, are signs that the child is 'cultured', and give many a parent the warm feeling of self-congratulation. These two ideas about the arts emerge from a thoroughly secular worldview, where the arts contain no serious meaning in themselves, with no power to shape the understanding. They are simply functional: they provide distraction, and they provide distinction.

In contrast to this is an authentically Christian view of the arts. In this view, the arts are formative, not only to one's love of the arts themselves, but to one's worldview. A Christian worldview, a Christian sensibility, or disposition, is powerfully shaped by art that emerged from such a Christian disposition (and, I might add, properly understood within that stream of understanding). The Christian imagination that provides a right interpretation of the discursive 'Bible facts' is shaped by artistic forms that are non-discursive in themselves. Before and behind cognition is affection, shaped by the imagination. As if we needed to defend why the arts are essential to a Christian imagination as we are describing it, let me simply list out three reasons.

First, the arts are analogical by nature. We have said the imagination understands the world by comparing, contrasting or otherwise analogizing the sensory experience that comes to it. This matter of analogy is the stock-in-trade of the arts. The various elements in art combine to abstract some idea, and then provide an analogy. The music, the painting, the poem, or the story uses its various elements to take some idea from reality, and say, "This is like that." Good art provides us with a sense of proportion: the artist felt a certain way about such an idea, and the experience is recreated for us. In other words, the artist suggests to us through his work how we should respond to such an idea, and what such an idea deserves.

Art mostly works in the abstract: it does not giving us concrete ideas like a population census or car-repair manual. But it gives us ideas nonetheless, and shapes our heart's response to those ideas. The arts reach the imagination directly, and more powerfully than logic and reason ever will. If you want your children to feel rightly toward God and His Word, then the arts provide much of that pre-cognitive disposition.

Second, the arts are essential to knowing transcendent realities. The universe is not merely a set of physical realities. We Christians also believe there are moral realities. That is, we believe there is such a thing as Truth. We believe that in God's universe, there is such as thing as the Good, and its opposite. Along with this, we believe there is such a thing as Beauty. God's glory is the quintessence of beauty, as many Scriptures attest. If the aim of our lives is to glorify God, we can say without hesitation that recognizing beauty is as important as recognizing truth and goodness. As surely as we would want our children to be able to judge a proposition to be true or false, we want them to judge something to be beautiful or ugly. Nor can the true, the good and the beautiful be neatly separated from one another. Recognizing beauty is fundamental to knowing the good God in truth. Good men do not love what is ugly. Lovers of truth regard beauty as good in itself. Fundamental to knowing the trinity of transcendentals is a right use of the arts.

Even non-Christians have recognised that the arts are perhaps our strongest and most direct link to the transcendent. The true, the good, and the beautiful are not 'facts' we collect in a test-tube; they are the realities behind the atoms that make up our universe. They are the transcendent realities above, beyond and behind immanent reality. The arts connect us to these realities. They represent these realities. They teach us ordinate responses to these realities. To dismiss or abuse the arts is to confine ourselves to mere physical reality, and become what Lewis called 'trousered apes'. If our children do not understand the arts as God gave them to us, they will suffer the fate of the Christian who tries to hang on to his faith by hunting for better and clearer 'biblical facts', while his imagination is ever tending towards anti-supernaturalism.

Third, God Himself gave His Word in artistic form. God could have given His Word as a technical manual, or as a long list of imperatives. Instead, the Bible itself is the master-work of imagination. The Bible is a work of art, in the literal sense of the term. Nearly a third of it is poetry, written by poetic geniuses like Isaiah, David, and Jeremiah. Another large section is narrative, redacted and edited in precise ways to weave a moving and gripping account of the story of God's glory. Apocalyptic books abound in imagery, mostly terrifying, but worlds away from a dry, discursive lecture. Even the Law is saturated with ceremonies and rituals rich in typology and imagery. The small section of epistolary literature is as close to discursive as it gets, but even there the language is loaded with imagery, metaphor and symbols: justification, redemption, propitiation, sanctification, and so forth. If God chose to give His Word to us in this form, what does that say about how important the arts are? If our children's artistic imaginations are dulled, they will certainly be at a cruel disadvantage when picking up the Word of God. Indeed, they may blindly fumble their way past all the beauty of the Word, trying to get to the 'facts', as if such exist apart from the form they are given in. If we believe the Word is where God is revealed to us, and the Word comes to us in artistic form, it is crucial that our children understand the arts for their own understanding of the Word.

To this we could add the fact that God has commanded the use of the arts in worship, and it is in worship that we come to know Him properly. Apart from a competent grasp of the arts, how will our children know if their responses to God are ordinate?

Parents need to know that the arts are not decorative. They are essential to knowing transcendent reality. And if so, we do well to consider some possibilities. What if your child's understanding of literature does not only determine if he enjoys Defoe and Dickens, but determines if he loves the Story: the Good News? What if her appreciation of Shakespeare, Herbert, or Donne is not simply a matter of enjoying the best verse of England, but affects her ability to enjoy the songs of Zion? What if his violin practice goes beyond acceptance into music school, and affects his entrance into Heaven?

Music

To shape a child's religious imagination means teaching him to rightly understand, use, and judge the arts. For a Christian parent, music is at the top of the list of the arts to be taught. Music is commanded in worship (Eph 5:19, Col 3:16), commended for worship (Ps 150), and has perhaps the greatest power of all the arts to shape the affections and transform the imagination.

How should a parent approach the teaching of this powerful imaginative art form? I commend to you a short but dense work: *Who Needs Classical Music?* by Julian Johnson[6]. Johnson argues persuasively that much of the problem with judging music for its meaning is how we have to come to use music: as a mood-maker, as background ambient sound, as a fashion symbol. When we view and use music like this, we empty it of its meaning, and destroy its ability to transform us. Music used this

---

6   New York, NY: Oxford University Press, 2002.

way can only reflect our current prejudices back to ourselves. Music becomes an aid to narcissism and an idolatry of surface appearances.

Serious music, art music, or 'classical' music, if you prefer, resists this treatment because of its form. Attempts are made today to make it fit into the world of pop, but it typically doesn't do well there, unless torn out of context, re-shaped, and played by a half-dressed temptress violin player.

One of our goals as parents is to help our children to judge music for itself: for its beauty, its form, and the ideas it is trying to persuade us of. They will certainly fail in this task if our culture's use of music as a disposable sonic anti-depressant becomes theirs. How can we resist this cultural momentum?

First, our children should each learn an instrument, as early as possible and until each one is competent. We do not leave reading or numeracy up to them as a 'personal choice', and since we expect them to mature into church members who are obedient to Ephesians 5:19, musical literacy ought to be compulsory. Learning an instrument is essential for grounding a child in the grammar and dialectic of music. For people who are commanded to sing psalms, hymns and spiritual songs, we should aim for nothing less than our children's sight-reading of the tunes in the hymnals.

Second, we should expose them to teaching tools

that help them to listen thoughtfully to great music. Leonard Bernstein's *Children's Classics*, which walks children through *Peter and the Wolf, Carnival of the Animals,* as well as his own *Young Person's Guide to the Orchestra,* is very helpful here.

Third, if we are to teach them to listen to and judge music for itself, we should set aside time to do nothing but listen to and experience serious music. If classical music simply plays in the background all the time, we teach our children to regard it as posh musical wallpaper, possessing the same arbitrary value usually assigned to pop music. Since few of us have enough power of concentration to stare thoughtfully at a speaker for an hour or more, this might mean purchasing some DVDs of orchestras performing great works, or watching them online. If possible, attending a concert is first prize. Even when very young, we can ask our children, "Is this happy or sad music?" "What should we feel when we hear this?" "What picture is he painting for us?" Humble beginnings maybe, but at least we are pointing our children to think with the music. The older our children are, the more sophisticated the criticism can become.

Fourth, it goes without saying that we want our children to become familiar with the musical tradition of both the West and the church. Though they will have a lifetime to experience these works, we want them to become more and more familiar with the musical conversation that has taken place over hundreds of years. This also means teaching them the history of music and hymnody, for art only makes sense within a tradition. If our children do not understand how music developed, they will not understand the conversation. And when the composers are deliberately opposing a Christian view of reality, this is a bad thing.

And finally, a word about the music your children will hear at church. If possible, avoid churches where the music offered to God suggests knowing God is like a dreamy icecapade, cruising the Blue Danube, or dizzily waltzing to His approaching return. Avoid churches where the music reminds one of being in a saloon in the Wild West before Sheriff Malone sidles in and breaks up the party. Avoid churches where the songs sung to God could double as tunes for a child's Nursery Rhyme CD, provide scene music for Disney cartoons, or work well as elevator music. Avoid churches where the music of worship could successfully assist roller-skaters, play-therapists or fussy infants at bedtime. Avoid churches where the music sounds like a poor mix of a garage band, *The Bangles* and really amateur *U2*-wannabes. Avoid churches where the music causes scrunchy-face worshippers to do their facial contortions. Avoid churches where the worshippers head-bang, thrash, and strum air-guitars, or where they applaud themselves, hoot and whistle after each song. Avoid churches where the music seems to cause the worshippers to enter various states of trance and to do odd and atypical things with their arms and hands. Avoid churches where the songs sung in Sunday School would make even Barney blush purpler with their inanity, and give the child the idea that praising God is a mixture of physical hyperactivity, weak comedy, and the display of the most juvenile and ridiculous impulses latent in human beings. I know this greatly pares down your choices, and some of this may be beyond your control. However, if you can find the rare exception, where the music helps form ordinate affection, you will be greatly aiding your child's view of God.

Poetry

Also, poetry appeals to the emotions, as does music, and like music, beautiful and rightly ordered poetry can habituate or train the soul to the right kind of internal movement. Familiarity with truly good poetry will encourage children to love the good, to hope for its victory, and to feel sad at its demise. The opposite habituation is very clear to see in children who watch or read stories in which the grotesque is taken for granted. They cease to be shocked by what is really disgusting. That is a great loss to the soul.

- Laura M. Berquist[7]

For a people whose Bible is one-thirds poetry, Christians are surprisingly dismissive of poetry. Taking their cue from the wider culture, many Christians see poetry meeting life only in odd places: the nonsense world of nursery rhymes, the rhyming lyrics of popular songs, and as an ornament at the end of a speech, movie or eulogy. They recognise that poetry exists in the Bible, and in their hymns and songs, but somehow these take on a special, functional use that distinguishes them from "other poetry". Rare is the modern Western Christian who sees poetry as ennobling, formative and vital to shaping the moral imagination.

I have already pointed out that much of the Word of God is in poetic form. Poetry provides analogies that expose our children to transcendent realities and convey right affections towards those realities. Poetry will "encourage children to love the good, to hope for its victory, and to feel sad at its demise."[8]

Laura Berquist, quoted above, writes, "Poetry is one of the forms of the beautiful that is relatively accessible to children. Children respond to patterns of sound and enjoy the rhythm of poetry, if they are introduced to it before someone tells them they shouldn't like it."[9] Since so much of God's Word is

7   *The Harp & Laurel Wreath* (San Francisco: Ignatius Press, 1999), 9.
8   *The Harp and Laurel Wreath*, 9.
9   Ibid., 8.

poetry, Christian parents ought to work hard to oppose the idea that poetry is boring, sissified or pretentious.

As in our discussion of music, there are preparatory steps that parents can take to ready their children for a lifelong love of poetry, and to lead up to the poetry of Scripture. At the ages we are talking about, our approach is mostly one of exposure to good poetry. Here and there, we might point out bad, trivial or useless poetry. We won't have to hunt for this; modern Sunday School songbooks typically provide a vast treasure-trove of such.

First, since children naturally chant and rhyme, parents can take advantage of this by teaching them to memorise nursery rhymes and simple poems. Berquist's book contains several poems by poets like Robert Louis Stevenson, A.A. Milne and G.K. Chesterton that young children can memorise.

Second, our children can learn very simple poems for worship. And here is where our ignorance of poetry has devastated us. Parents (and many pastors) confuse the idea of a simple song with the idea of a trivial song. Songs that are trivial in metaphor, comical in metre, and ridiculous in content are seen as "age-appropriate". We seem to have lost the ability to judge between a simple, helpful poem like *Jesus Loves Me*, and a nonsensical one like *Jesus Wants Me For a Sunbeam*.

I don't want to soil this chapter with examples of foolish Sunday School songs. Your mind has perhaps been stained enough by long-term exposure to them. Instead, consider some poems written for children by Isaac Watts and Charles Wesley. Watch how two masters could combine simplicity and profundity, teaching without trivialising.

Duty to God and our neighbour – Isaac Watts

Love God with all your soul and strength.
With all your heart and mind;
And love your neighbour as yourself:
Be faithful, just, and kind.

Hosanna – Isaac Watts

To God the Father, God the Son
And God the Spirit, Three In One
Be Honour, Praise and Glory Be Giv'n
By All on Earth and All in Heav'n

Hymn XXXVI – Charles Wesley

Children have a right to sing
Praises to their Infant-King,
Tell how Christ the holy child
God and man hath reconcil'd.

Here is where we can help even our younger children to judge wisely. When they come across a foolish song, a limerick for Jesus, or some inanity posing as age-appropriate worship, we can ask our children, "What does that poem make us feel? Should we feel like that about God? Is it right to compare Jesus to that? Where does that song belong?" Expose them to the good; ridicule and shame the evil. Yes, we want our children to have a strong and healthy contempt for ugly and useless poetry, particularly when it profanes God's name. We want the metaphors, rhythms and rhymes of good poetry to be embedding themselves deep in their imaginations before they have come to understand why they are true, good and beautiful.

Third, even young children can learn stanzas from certain hymns. Hymns which young children readily memorize are *Holy, Holy, Holy, I Sing the Mighty Power of God, All Creatures of Our God and King, The Doxology, All Praise to Thee My God This Night*. The melodies of these hymns aid memorisation, and these hymns contain the kind of poetry with which we want to furnish our children's imaginations.

Literature

When we discuss the Christian imagination, people tend to think of fantasy, story-books and films. Those parents who agree that the imagination ought to be shaped often think in two directions: limit the SNVL, and find 'good Christian themes'. That is, cut out (or down) the Sex-Nudity-Violence-Language element, and find stories that seem to preach Christianity.

If we are to shape the moral and religious imaginations of our children, so that they are favourably disposed towards the gospel, we must give attention to belletristic literature – stories, narratives, and tales that reach the imagination.

Just as inferior music and poetry can warp the imagination, so too can literature. The characters can be flat and sub-human. The stories can be book-long clichés, doing nothing more that reinforcing slothful thinking about the world. The morality may be nothing more than platitudinous sermonizing. But make no mistake, when complete, the child's view of what is noble, courageous, worthy, beautiful, upright has been affected. His affections have been shaped, for good or ill.

I have witnessed the sad result of children fed a steady diet of evangelical trash-novels and saccharine-stories: girls who would have called Jesus' actions in the Temple 'naughty', boys who think that Jesus was a pacifist hippie, and steal a guilty indulgence in some play-fighting now and then. I have seen the consequence of parents without discernment in this area in their twentysomethingyear-old, and truly the sins of the fathers are passed on.

Let me encourage you to read George MacDonald's article, "The Fantastic Imagination." MacDonald reminds us what a true tale does, and how, and for whom. The best stories do not convince as a logical treatise does, they awaken and arouse. Their images do not merely meet our expectations or reinforce our prejudices, but provoke us, challenge us, and change us. Talking vegetables, repentant firemen and Post-Rapture Survival Teams seldom do these things. Nor do the best stories simply provide distraction, escape or amusement. They lead us to step away from the material world for a moment, view it through the moral imagination of the tale, and return with better eyes. They present us with another world, with its own laws. When told well, the tale and its world give us windows into our own.

So let MacDonald be a starting point for tales to read to your children old enough to understand: *The Princess and the Goblin*, *The Princess and Curdie*, and then go on to sample his others. Sift through and read Grimm's and then Andersen's Fairy Tales. Andrew Lang's books are in the public domain, and you won't run out of fairy tales there. Then there is C. S. Lewis's *Narnia*, and for the older children, his space trilogy. Tolkien's *The Hobbit* will be palatable for some younger children, as will *Smith of Wootton Major*, *Leaf By Niggle*, and *Farmer Giles of Ham*. E. S. Nesbit, T. H. White, and Roger Lancelyn Green are others worth considering, and by the time you're through all those, your child will hopefully be reading himself, and have a taste for well-crafted stories. Even some of the mythology of pagan cultures – with some parental guidance – can be helpful to a forming imagination.

Michael O'Brien's *A Landscape With Dragons* defends the importance of a Christian literary imagination in our children, and the appendix contains hundreds of recommended titles, though we do not endorse his Romanism.

Again, we want our children to do more than passively imbibe music, poetry or literature. We want them to become judges of good and evil, beautiful and ugly, true and false. Probably more than any other art form, stories lead children to weigh, to order, to judge, to arrange, as they make sense of the moral universe of the stories they hear. And if those stories are sentimental, incoherent, misleading, superficial, or propagandising, our children emerge from those stories with disordered imaginations. How much SNVL they contained becomes a secondary concern. We want them to judge the characters, to oppose and cheer, to compare choices, to distinguish good from evil (sometimes in the same character), to weigh motives and actions and consequences. Our goal is not to 'find the meaning' in some pedantic and cruelly mechanistic way, but to allow a story that emerged from a Christian (or pre-

Christian) imagination to have its shaping effect upon us.

For as we do this, we are preparing our children for the Greatest Story Ever Told. We are helping them to make sense of the story of Creation, the Fall, The Plan of Redemption, The Incarnation, and the Kingdom. And since this is the true story of reality, we want our children reading and hearing the "truest" tales man has told.

Plastic Arts

Non-literary and non-musical arts powerfully shape the imagination. Since the media triumph of television and film, these arts have taken a back seat. Only art aficionados seem to go to galleries any more, and the popular use of this kind of imagination has become an almost exclusively decorative or utilitarian one. Regardless, such works of imagination can powerfully prepare our children for the gospel if rightly used.

Let me suggest that a parent might acquaint himself with the meaning of art through books like Rookmaaker's *Modern Art and the Death of a Culture* or Tom Wolfe's *The Painted Word*. Once again, the crucial matter is judgement – teaching children to weigh, order, arrange, compare, contrast, and value.

As far as educating the imagination of a child might go, some helpful courses are available which help in terms of understanding and appreciation. Apart from visits to your local gallery, some books mentioned in the appendix of this book may help in terms of exposure to the great canon of Western works.

One popular use of art that seems to get a free pass from Christian parents and pastors is the art used in children's Bibles, Sunday school material, and other teaching material aimed at children. According to the age-appropriate gurus, the pictures and artwork here must be comical, colourful, or cartoonish. Little do they realize that such artwork stands for certain ideas in our culture. They are commonly used for comical themes, sentimentalised visions of life (everything is sunny and smiley-faced), and are iconic for what is childish. The purveyors of this material are thinking like true populist evangelicals: the gospel is for everyone, and using artwork that our culture recognises as childish is how we make the gospel palatable, attractive and comprehensible to children. That idea may certainly come across, and parents may be thrown off by the interest and curiosity that their children show. Sadly, what they miss are the ideas that come along with that immediate appeal: that the gospel may as well be a funny story, that Bible stories are as fictional as their other storybooks, that the giggles and awws they feel and express in those stories fits perfectly when encountering God. Worst of all, the maturing child begins to think that if depictions of biblical stories are childish, then the ideas they teach must be also. It is a strange vision of Christian education that thinks children are better off if the realism of the Bible is translated into smiley-faced soldiers around Joshua, happy-faced lions with Daniel, and bloodless, goreless, painless depictions of Scriptural narratives.

Another of the plastic arts that seems forgotten by evangelicals is architecture. Sadly, most of our children must attend church in buildings that could double as shops, gymnasiums, or offices, and the idea of a consecrated space designed with worshippers in mind is seemingly rejected as money-wasting by the liturgically-minded.

Not many parents (or pastors, for that matter) are in a position to singlehandedly change the architecture of the church they attend. It might be worthwhile to schedule visits with your children to some buildings of beauty, be they places of worship or not. Again, for help here, see the appendix.

And then a final word about theatre, though it is not one of the plastic arts. Theatre, whether on stage, television or movie screen is a form of art that many Christian parents express concern about. Whether their worry is the amount of hours used watching, or the content, or the deleterious effect it seems to have on concentration, rare is the parent who thinks that theatre is an unmitigated blessing. Since convictions regarding the propriety of theatre for Christians range widely, let me give three observations, and leave it to your judgement.

1) Until the 20th century, the church nearly universally condemned it. Perhaps their condemnation was short-sighted and partial, but you ought to hear their arguments before you write them all off as invalid.

2) The concrete and immediate nature of theatre is overwhelming to the affections. One is not observing, reflecting and feeling; one is reacting: immersed in the action, and often cheering for what you would not otherwise, desiring something you would otherwise know as wrong. All the more so with children, who are learning to feel and judge. Movies tend to hand them those judgements like a doctor's rubber hammer gets a knee to extend. Best that those judgements are sound before you expose your children to them.

3) Next to theatre, arts like poetry, literature, the plastic arts, and serious music with its abstract nature, simply cannot compete, in the mind of a child. Younger children gravitate away from prolonged reflection anyway. They dislike abstractions and opaque metaphors. When a story is played before them, with all the sights and sounds provided in an immersive experience, their appetite for theatre strengthens, and their disdain for the other arts may likewise grow. Perhaps this is the fallacy of false cause, and theatre and the other arts may in fact safely co-exist. If not, however, any

appetite which destroys the love of poetry, literature or serious music is an evil appetite, for this will certainly harm their love of the Word of God. If God's people need the poetical eye for meditation of God's Word, best that they not become people impatient with perception, concentration and reflection.

I would suggest parents treat this medium with caution, and work hard to foster love for the other arts.

VIII

The Christian Tradition

No poet, no artist of any art, has his complete meaning alone. His significance, his appreciation is the appreciation of his relation to the dead poets and artists. You cannot value him alone; you must set him, for contrast and comparison, among the dead. I mean this as a principle of aesthetic, not merely historical, criticism.

- T.S. Eliot, "Tradition and the Individual Talent"[10]

Living in a culture requires that we understand broadly agreed-upon symbolic conventions. To speak of culture at all presumes that meaning has a validity beyond individual interpretations. Meaning that is defined purely by the individual has nothing to do with the idea of culture. This relationship, between subjective expression and social meaning, is rooted in language, with its tension between the social demands of language and the individual speech acts through which we enter into it.

- Julian Johnson, *Who Needs Classical Music?*[11]

---

10   In *Selected Essays* (Rahway, NJ: Harcourt, Brace & Co., 1932).

When we expose our children to imaginative works of great beauty, we must not suppose that these works can have their full effect in isolation. Your child's understanding of language does not come by randomly reading out multisyllabic words to him from a dictionary. He gains it through using words, and being exposed to meanings over a long process of time. It is as he learns language within his culture that he understands word meanings.

Eliot reminds us that no artist's work is properly understood in isolation. It is understood when considered as part of a long conversation, extending over hundreds of years. Artists, poets, musicians and writers use forms that are understood in a culture, and develop them. When we become aware of this conversation, and the various paths it took, we better understand the individual works of art. Apart from this, we listen to symphonies, view sculptures and read poems and literature the way an English speaker might hear a French oration. It might sound beautiful, and the speaker might guess at certain emotions being expressed, but comprehension is severely limited.

If we are concerned about pre-evangelism, that is, preparing our children's imaginations to favourably judge, weigh, value and understand the gospel and biblical doctrine, then we must be concerned about exposing our children to the tradition that emerged from Christianity. Such a tradition was informed by biblical categories, and went on to express Christian ideas in language, music, poetry, architecture, painting, and literature. We cannot expect Christian works of imagination to work on the imagination like two aspirin work on the bloodstream. We must understand them as parts of a long conversation, as parts of a Christian culture.

Our great problem in this regard is that secularisation has led to Christian churches existing with little connection to the hundreds of years of Christian culture that went before us. Churches have either tried to baptise secular culture with Christian ideas, or tried to hold on to traditional Christian culture in small islands, disconnected from the true transmission and development that culture requires. Ours is a difficult day, with an evil choice.

Though we cannot just 'adopt' a culture that is no longer ours, we can expose our children to it. We can teach them of the culture that emerged from professing Christianity, and the forms it developed to express its worldview. Douglas Wilson, in *The Case for Classical Christian Education*, quotes Christopher Dawson:

> For the educated person cannot play his full part in modern life unless he has a clear sense of the nature and achievements of Christian culture: how Western civilization became Christian

and how far it is Christian today and in what ways it has ceased to be Christian: in short, a knowledge of our Christian roots and of the abiding Christian elements in Western culture.[12]

No one is claiming that the West was completely colonised by the gospel. What is clear is that in the providence of God, the West was shaped by Christian ideas, and the West gave expression to Christian ideas in its poetry, music, literature, liturgies, architecture, and jurisprudence. Therefore, one of the goals in shaping the Christian imagination is to expose our children to the progress of Western history: the histories of the classical civilizations that influenced the church, the history of the church through the ages, the history of the West in the Middle Ages, through the Renaissance, and into the dark period that atheists so conceitedly called the Enlightenment. Once again, Wilson:

> At the same time, Western culture receives the emphasis it does because this is the culture in which the Christian faith has made the greatest advances. Western civilization is not synonymous with the kingdom of God, but the histories of the two entities are so intertwined that one cannot be understood apart from the other. Try to

12   Wheaton, IL: Crossway, 2003, 128.

imagine a decent history of the West that made no reference to Christianity or a church history that made no mention of Charlemagne or Constantine.[13]

In teaching this history, we are teaching more than names and dates. We are teaching the progress of doctrine, the formation of metaphors, the meaning of the analogies that became the shared information of Christian culture. More importantly, these metaphors and analogies became the shared sentiment towards the things of God, the shared affections toward the worship of God. Put simply, our children must become literate in the culture that Christianity developed, if they are to be properly shaped by works of the Christian imagination.

---

13   Ibid., 84.

IX

Language, Thinking and Christian Education

To understand reality, a child must think. Thinking that brings understanding is not the thinking that a cow does when it notices a car passing its pasture. It is the kind of thinking about ideas. To think about ideas, a child must know language. Language is the technology of thought.

Language, as we are using it here, does not refer to a vast set of names about the world. Chimps and dogs can be taught certain names and verbal commands. Language as the activity of God's image-bearers is a matter of making predications, statements about things in the world. Real language does not simply name things, it tells us something about them. Only when we are telling – describing, valuing, explaining, relating, comparing, contrasting – are we using language as persons made in God's image.

Human language is an extraordinarily fine tool for this task. We can explain actions in the past, present, or future. We can suggest the action was conditional, imperative, or definite. We can describe the action as progressive, completed or incomplete.

We can make a subject responsible for an action or the recipient of it. We can choose from a bewildering variety of synonyms to find the particular shade of meaning we need. Our world of ideas, from the child's first book to the most obscure philosophical textbook, exists only because we are able to use language.

What happens to the soul whose technology of thought is broken with flawed grammar and a skeletal vocabulary? His range of ideas is immediately limited. His potential to weigh, discriminate, judge, contrast, and make the kind of fine distinctions necessary to wisdom is greatly diminished. His disordered language reflects disordered ideas, and disordered ideas do not represent the orderly universe God made.

If we wish our children to embrace the reality of God according to Scripture, we must prepare them to do so with careful attention to language. Not only do we want them to be competent readers of Scripture, we want them to be competent thinkers. They will only think clearly when they have received more than passing attention to grammar.

Here I insert my preference for an education that drills children in grammar and syntax. When the connections between words are understood, a clarity of ideas emerges. When the child thinks that his words just refer to things, he is less particular about weighing ideas, and all the more likely to be tossed to and fro with every wind of doctrine.

It is no secret that serious discourse is almost dead. Read the arguments in the comments section of most blogs. Listen to political rhetoric. Read columnists, and yes, sadly, listen to more than a few sermons. Precision of thought has been replaced by platitudes, unchallenged assumptions and fictions. Disciplined reasoning and coherent discourse has been replaced by wild gesticulating, and wide-eyed defences of cherished prejudices.

In the resulting fragility, the truths and ideas of the gospel may not be as clear and reasonable to young minds, if those young minds have not been taught to think clearly and reason well. If we are careless about language, we throw our children to the lions of pluralism and incoherent discourse, and possibly cripple their ability to rightly view the ideas of the gospel.

We will only see this kind of approach to reading, writing, and thinking if our children have a truly Christian education.

More Than Piety

"The purpose of a Christian education would not be merely to make men and women pious Christians: a system which aimed too rigidly at this end alone would become only obscurantist. A Christian education must primarily teach people to be able to think in Christian categories." So said T.S. Eliot.

The great myth of education in the Western world is that it is possible to have a purely 'secular' education. Christians have typically bought this lie, thinking that secular education will give their children value-free, neutral 'facts' about the world, to which the parents can season and mix in some Bible facts every Sunday. They think schools are simply information mills, cranking out facts that will equip the child to one day 'get a job'.

Interestingly, very few other religions agree. Orthodox Jews educate their children in their own schools. Devout Muslims begin their own schools. Hindus, Buddhists, and others who take their faith seriously see to it that their young are educated in schools of their own making. They do so because they do not believe that secular schools are amoral information factories. Secular schools are also religious schools.

Undeniably, secularism is a religion. The religion of secularism preaches that while God may exist, He doesn't matter for the 'realities of life'. Therefore, your devotion to Him must be something 'very personal', and never preached as true for anyone besides yourself. All religions are equally true, in that they are merely personal choices for your own happiness. Therefore, all religions must be equally represented and be given the same space at the table.

As much as secularism postures as non-religious, it is profoundly religious. It has a god ("Progress"), a grand myth to explain life ("Evolution"), a standard of value ("human well-being"), and faith ("objective analysis"). It rejects the centrality of God's Revelation in the Bible, dethrones God as the source of ultimate reality, and denies human sinfulness.

"Secular" education is by no means a non-religious education. It is simply an education in the religion of secularism. If we send our children to school, the question is not *if* the school will be religious, it is *which* religion it will educate the children in. What then is a Christian education?

A Christian Philosophy of Education

Christian education is not a veneer of Bible facts lightly painted over the furniture of secularism. Christian education is discipleship.

Discipleship is the goal of the Great Commission (Mt 28:19-20). Christ desires that we would be instruments in His miraculous work of turning rebels into worshippers. A disciple loves God supremely, loves his neighbour as himself and loves creation as God loves it. The disciple must be supernaturally regenerated, and then begin a life-long process of instruction and obedience in the local church.

Christian education is nothing less than a substantial part of this instruction and training in righteousness.

To understand how a Christian philosophy of education differs from a secular one, we need to point out what a Christian education is *not*.

Christian education is not primarily preparation for a career. Christian education is not chiefly concerned with giving a person a set of 'marketable skills'. Though these are important, and a good education will certainly lay the foundation for these, Christian education is not an exercise in equipping our children to 'get a job'. Knowledge is not a tool to be exploited for sheer financial gain. Rightly used, it will certainly provide (Proverbs 24:4), but knowledge is a gift from God to be wisely managed, not an aid to financial mercenaries.

Christian education is not moralism added to secular knowledge. Christian education is not merely a moral lesson connected to the curriculum, or Bible verses scattered through the otherwise-secular coursework. It is not merely prayer in the morning, a sermon at assembly and a Bible Education class. These might satisfy some parents' desires for 'good moral values to be instilled', but it still falls short of true Christian education. Disciples are not created by adding a few moral lessons to secular curricula.

Christian education is not mimicking secular education with allusions to Christianity. Like the home, a school is always faced with the temptation to live lives indistinguishable from its secular counterparts. To borrow from the world's approach to learning, instruction, discipline, relationships between teachers and scholars, parental involvement, sports and extramurals, and then add Christian mottoes, vision statements and Bible verses hardly qualifies as Christian education. Cross-carrying, self-denying Christians do not emerge from twelve years of secular education, simply because the school had a Christian vision statement.

To summarise, Christian education is an exercise in *antithesis*, as Douglas Wilson puts it. That is, Christian education stands in opposition to the values and beliefs of the age. It holds that the earth is the Lord's (Ps 24:1), and the whole world lies in darkness. Consequently, Christian education aims to teach Christians to see all of life through God's eyes – including maths, geography, poetry, and soccer. Christian education holds that there is also an *unbelieving* way to view maths, geography, poetry and soccer. Christian education stands in antithesis to worldly views that oppose God (2 Cor 10:5-6). Christian education begins with God as the only One who can make sense of human knowledge, and His Word as the infallible record of His mind. Christian education begins with God's glory as the highest end, God's Word as the final authority and ultimate love for Him as the chief goal. This antithetical approach affects the curriculum, the discipline, the way knowledge is taught, and myriads of other situations.

Christian education stands in contrast to secular education by its four pursuits. Christian education pursues four goals that distinguish it from secular thinking.

First, the pursuit of wisdom. Wisdom is nothing like the fact-collecting approach of modern science. A wise man's head is not bursting with disconnected facts gathered from the sciences, the humanities or other areas of knowledge. Wisdom is the skill to understand knowledge gained from God's world, and to apply it for God's glory. When you are wise, you see life from God's perspective, and turn those perspectives into practical obedience. A life of holiness – the life of a disciple – follows from a heart of wisdom.

Christian education is not an exercise in collecting facts to turn them into money. Christian education is the pursuit of knowledge, understanding, and wisdom, to become more like Christ. That's why at the heart of wisdom, and therefore at the heart of Christian education, is the fear of the Lord (Prov 1:7, 9:10). For this reason, worship is at the heart of Christian education. Only young worshippers will properly construe the knowledge they gain, and turn it into wisdom. A Christian school that ignores worship is not a Christian school in deed. Before all else, Christian education seeks to create reverent disciples – people who fear God, and want to gain His perspective on all of life. Christian ethics and a life of applying

Scripture to situations emerge from true Christian education. Christian education has succeeded when it has created people who are skilled at applying God's Word to God's world.

Secondly, the pursuit of a Christian worldview. A worldview is not one window for your mind to look out from. Your worldview is the lens through which you see everything. Worldview is how you understand the past, the present, and the future. Worldview is your standard of judgement: what is good, true and beautiful. Worldview defines God, others, the world, and yourself. Worldview is your idea of reality, your understanding of what is real.

Christian education aims at nothing less than giving children a thoroughly Christian worldview. Not satisfied with teaching poetry, literature, geography, biology, history or business economics lightly seasoned with Bible verses, it insists that every domain of knowledge be understood as God sees it, and used as God commands it. This means that Christian education has a uniquely Christian *epistemology*. That is, Christian education believes a right way of knowing exists, and pursues this. This means at least three things.

First, it sees God's Word as central to understanding, authoritative and final in authority. The Bible provides the framework to understand all knowledge in the world. Scripture is the primary grid through which to view reality. A Christian education does more than pepper secular knowledge with Bible verses, it re-interprets all knowledge through biblical filters.

Second, it educates the imagination. Christian education will give attention to those things that reach and shape the imagination directly: music, poetry, literature, art.

Third, it educates within a tradition. A Christian understanding of the world does not emerge out of thin air. Christians do not come up with the faith afresh in every generation. Christians hand the faith on to others, who then hand it on to others (2 Tim 2:2). This means a stream of understanding has flowed and increased from the day of the apostles. Christian education steps into that stream and educates with that momentum behind it. This means understanding the history of Christianity and Christian thought, alongside the study of Western culture and thought.

Thirdly, the pursuit of sound thinking. Because no lie can be used in the service of the truth, a Christian education cannot accept untruths at any point. If knowledge is disordered, wrongly applied, or misunderstood, it deceives. Christian education is fastidious about clarity, logical validity, and sound reason. For this reason, Christian education is exacting when it comes to language. Language expresses ideas, and when the language is disordered, the ideas are wrong. Indeed, Christian education even presses for a study of parent languages to our own, to increase our precision in language, and expand our dexterity. It sees importance in studying the original languages of Scripture.

Similarly, Christian education prizes logic and reason. Sound argumentation, inductive and deductive reasoning and formal logic are needful for a Christian to answer the thought-bombs of Satan (2 Cor 10:5-6). Christian education sees value in subjects like formal logic, mathematics, and geometry, not merely for practical value, but for the rigorous logic and reasoning power they give to the mind.

Fourthly, the pursuit of vocation. Christian education desires to shape disciples, not merely equip careerists. Nevertheless, Christian education cares that its scholars fulfil their callings. First Corinthians 7:18-23 teaches that every Christian has a calling, or vocation. God appoints these stations in life, and fulfilment comes in pursuing and accomplishing one's callings.

A Christian education worth the name will pursue wisdom, a Christian worldview, sound thinking and vocation. The child who experiences such an education, be it at home or at a Christian school, will certainly be in a better place, from a pre-evangelism point of view, than his secular counterpart.

X

Conclusion

In considering how the imagination of a child is shaped, we have discussed parental piety, family roles in the home, routines, rituals (such as family worship, corporate worship, and special events), manners, art (such as music, poetry, literature, the plastic arts) the Christian tradition, and language and education itself. When considered together, shaping the imagination is not an activity here or there, but the bulk of life lived as a family, with its connections to church and school. In the words of Deuteronomy 6 again, we shape our children to love God when we rise up and when we lie down, when we go and when we return. The goal is nothing short of how a child understands and judges reality itself. A child's interpretation of the world does not come through the objective sensory data supplied by the eyes and ears. Interpretation and understanding comes through images – images supplied by example, exposure, art, history and language.

To this, we could mention other matters which shape one's picture of God, oneself and the world. Anthony Esolen, in *Ten Ways to Destroy the Imagination of Your Child*, mentions matters like play, outdoors life and love of nature, and working with one's hands. Kent Hughes, in *Disciplines of a Godly Family*, repeats these and adds activities such as travel, hobbies and athletics. While these are not as formative as the matters we have considered, they still play a role. Remember, our goal is not the secularists' shallow vision of a 'well-rounded child' (whatever that is); we Christians hope to use all lawful means to shape our children's idea of reality.

Certainly, as I said at the beginning, I assume that we will teach the children the gospel. I assume we will catechise them thoroughly, saturate them in biblical doctrine, and immerse them in discipleship materials. The problem at hand is why, in spite of all this happening, so many turn away from God.

If a child's image of God, the world, and himself is fundamentally different to that portrayed in the Scriptures, not only will he think wrongly about God, himself and the world, but he will *feel* wrongly about them. His response to the universe will be one of wrong desires. These wrong desires will warp his thinking, and lead him to all the wrong conclusions. Romans 1:18-32 will play itself out in a similar fashion in his life.

Let me put it in everyday terms. If he imagines God as a granddad, the world as a bank to be plundered, and himself as a preciously good and lovable person, you will be hard-pressed to tell him that he is a sinner deserving death, that he has abused creation, and that God will judge him. He will reason that God can be trifled with, or that He may be ignored altogether. He will feel little awe towards God, little fear of judgement, and little joy at the thought of grace. And though he may have heard the gospel hundreds of times, (and possibly 'prayed the prayer') he will announce that he is 'agnostic' when he is nineteen. Parents will weep, pastors will shake their heads and counsel more prayer, and everyone will insist upon the need for more programs in church. Peers will be blamed, conversations will rue the movies and music of our day, but it will all amount to more excuses for another soul lost. If we are serious about our children's souls, we must become serious about the problem of the imagination.

Parents are responsible for helping to form and shape a child's overall mental map of reality. If they neglect to do so, there is no telling how the child will interpret the 'facts' of the gospel. Those facts are not autonomous, and the miracle of regeneration is not usually accomplished without the Spirit's use of means. Jesus might have turned water into wine, but He had some servants fill the water pots first. In the case of a child's regeneration, parents are those means, filling the water pots, shaping the imagination so that the Spirit will make use of that favourable disposition towards the Christian message.

I am a parent. I know that nothing except the undeserved grace of God can regenerate my children and keep them faithful. But I also know that the

Spirit uses means. For that reason, I wish to use as many of the means discussed in this book to shape my children's idea of God, themselves and the world. I do not think that the gospel truths will convert unless they are correctly seen, which is to say, correctly imagined. So I labour to prepare the hearts of my children to see the unseen as well as possible, so that the quickening Spirit may open their eyes to Christ. I see this shaping of their imagination as Elijah's preparation of the altar. I will do all I can, and trust God to send the fire.

Appendix A
Resources for Parents

Some helpful, not infallible, guides.

Imagination in General

* "The Fantastic Imagination" – George MacDonald. An essay that prefaced MacDonald's *Fairy Tales*. In the public domain.

* "The Ethics of Elfland", chapter in *Orthodoxy* – G.K. Chesterton. In the public domain.

* *Ten Ways to Destroy the Imagination of Your Child* – Anthony Esolen. Wilmington, DE: ISI Books, 2010.

Family Roles

* *Building Strong Families* – Dennis Rainey (ed.) Wheaton, IL: Crossway, 2002.

* *Gospel-Powered Parenting* – William P Farley. Philipsburg, NJ: P&R Publishing Company, 2009.

* *Shepherding a Child's Heart* – Tedd Tripp. Wapwallopen, PA: Shepherd Press, 1995.

Routines

* *Disciplines of a Godly Family* – Kent & Barbara Hughes. Wheaton, IL:

Crossway, 2004.

* *For the Family's Sake* – Susan Schaeffer Macaulay. Wheaton, IL: Crossway,

1999.

Rituals

* *Raising a Modern-Day Knight* – Robert Lewis. Carol Stream, IL: Tyndale House, 2007.

* *Treasuring God in Our Traditions* – Noel Piper . Wheaton, IL: Crossway, 2007.

Art

Music

* *Who Needs Classical Music* ?– Julian Johnson. New York, NY: Oxford University Press, 2002.

* *Children's Classics* – Leonard Bernstein. Sony, 1998.

* Kevin Bauder, in his article "Start Them Young"(*In the Nick of Time,* April 27, 2012, online article: http://www.centralseminary.edu/resources/nick-of-time/in-the-nick-of-time-archive/364-start-them-young), lists several works appropriate to begin children's musical appreciation:

Sergei Prokofiev's *Peter and the Wolf*

Camille Saint Saëns' *Carnival of the Animals*

Benjamin Britten's *Young Person's Guide to the Orchestra.*

Tchaikovsky's *Overture Solonnelle "1812."*

Beethoven's *Symphony No. 6*

Mussorgsky's *Pictures at an Exhibition*

Smetana's *The Moldau*

Brahm's *Hungarian Dances*

Mendelssohn's *Songs Without Words*

Handel's *Water Music* and *Fireworks Music*

Selections from Tchaikovsky's *Nutcracker*

Poetry

* *The Harp & Laurel Wreath* – Laura M. Berquist. San Francisco: Ignatius Press, 1999.

* *Divine and Moral Songs For Children*– Isaac Watts. In the public domain, and available online.

* *Hymns for Children* – Charles Wesley. In the public domain, and available online.

Suggested hymns to teach young children:

Jesus Loves Me

Love God With All Your Soul and Strength

All Creatures of Our God and King

I Sing the Mighty Power of God

Holy, Holy, Holy

When I Survey the Wondrous Cross

Come thou Fount

O God, Our Help in Ages Past

O Worship the King

All Praise to Thee, My God, This Night

Be Thou My Vision

Literature

* *A Landscape With Dragons* – Michael O' Brien. San Francisco: Ignatius Press, 1998.

Plastic Arts

* *Art: Over 2,500 Works from Cave to Contemporary* – Andrew Graham-Dixon New York, NY: DK Publishing, 2008.

* *Discovering Great Artists: Hands-On Art for Children in the Styles of the Great Masters* – MaryAnn F. Kohl. Bellingham, WA: Bright Ring Publishing, 1996.

* *Modern Art and the Death of a Culture* – H.R. Rookmaaker. Wheaton, IL: Crossway, 1994.

* *The Painted Word* – Tom Wolfe. New York, NY: Picardor, 1975.

* *The Story of Architecture* – Jonathan Glancey. New York, NY: DK Publishing, 2000.

Education

* *The Abolition of Man* – C.S. Lewis. New York, NY: HarperCollins, 1974.

* *The Case for Classical Christian Education* – Douglas Wilson. Wheaton, IL: Crossway, 2003.

* *The Lost Tools of Learning* – Dorothy Sayers. Essay in the public domain.

Appendix B

Ten Ways To Raise a Secularist

Webster's defines *secularism* as "indifference to or rejection or exclusion of religion and religious considerations." Judging by the expressions on the faces of young people during worship in many churches, we are doing quite well at raising a generation of robust secularists. To help parents along in this task, here are ten suggestions:

1) Attend a church where God rests lightly upon the worshippers. If the church does not know the difference between worship and entertainment, then this is sure to happen, and you should make such a church your spiritual home. Make sure that the programs (and there should be many of these) and ministries mostly emphasise *fun* as the supreme good. After Sunday School, ask your children, "Did you have fun?" Make sure the level of fun-making becomes more sophisticated as the children get older. During church, shrug off any efforts by the pastors to involve you in reflection, repentance, humility or adoration. Let your children see your impatience and restlessness with that kind of thing. If it continues, speak to the leadership and inform them of the wrong direction they are going with worship.

2) Treat the Lord's Day as a tiresome chore. Arrive at church, proceed with the formalities, and then get home for the *good stuff*: lunch, computer games, and ideally, some TV or movies. Don't mention the sermon at home, and definitely avoid any display of emotion in speaking of how the revelation of God affected you.

3) Fill the home, and the car, and the schedule with noise. That is, fill your children's lives with continual distraction: cartoons, lightweight sitcoms and movies, sports, computer games and the like. Keep everyone entertained from moment to moment, and keep meditation, silence and reflection far from your home.

4) Let your child's peers be his cultural mentors. Let other children define for him what is to be prized, valued, loved and treasured. Do this by making sure the bulk of his time is not spent with you, and when it is, don't bother to tell him what you think is true and good and beautiful. When he appears to be taking on the sullen, sceptical, and cynical attitude of his peers, you know you're making progress.

5) Fill his mind and his life with pop culture: pop music, movies, and TV. Let him be shaped by songs that trivialise the human condition, stories that evoke good feelings but forbid reflection, and generally art that the child enjoys without having to reflect, learn or struggle to understand. Make sure his whimsical feelings direct and form his tastes, and don't ever,

ever, force him to listen to serious music, learn an instrument, read good poetry and literature or go to an art gallery. Remember, you want to keep central to him his love of himself; therefore, anything that challenges him to enter into another person's world is bad. If he doesn't like something, let him know that it is bad, and if he likes it, it is good.

6) Don't teach him to compare and criticise things for their goodness, truth or beauty. If he develops any ability in this area, he will be developing the tools for worship, and that's not what you want. Ideally, find some nicely mixed-up forms – pop music posing as worship, juvenile poems posing as worship, cartoons and movies posing as Christian, and kitsch religious artwork. Once worship and self-gratifying entertainment are mixed up, he'll never be able to pull them apart, and will default to entertainment.

7) Celebrate the idols of our culture: sports, cars, technology, toys, brand-name clothes, great meals, and popular entertainments. Talk about these with enthusiasm and excitement, spend your money on them liberally, and let your children see that here is where your soul takes repose and finds delight. Rejoice together in your material acquisitions, reserve your highest words of praise for sports stars, and drool over catalogues, car shows and coming attractions. Involve your children in a pursuit of these things from their earliest years, so that they

know that these are the things that truly matter. Set it up so the highlight of the week is 'movie night', speak of it with anticipation, visibly show your delight when it comes, and surround it with all kinds of comfort ceremonies.

8) Keep his eyes glued to a screen of sorts: phone, iPad, computer, TV – it doesn't matter what kind. This will keep him away from seeing the works of God's hands, particularly the sky or the intricacy of growing and living things. Ideally, don't travel, but if you must, make sure that your car has a TV, the destination has satellite TV, and that he brings his screen with him.

9) Let him be careless about words and language. Clear ideas require clear thought, which requires precise language. You don't want this; you want your child to live in a vague, blurry world of contradictory notions and ideas. Vocabulary and diction are some of the *techne* of worship, so make sure he uses incoherent grammar, rejects clear definition, prefers slang, and never learns to write his thoughts out coherently.

10) Avoid all forms of manners, etiquette or everyday beauty in the home. These kinds of things teach him to think of appropriateness, order and decency (which belong to worship), to say nothing of the fact that they elevate his existence from the merely physical and material. Let informality seem natural and 'real', and let all custom, ritual and form

seem like hypocrisy and phoniness. In fact, tell him it is so.

Do this consistently for around, say, twenty years, and I can nearly guarantee you that by that time, your children will be thorough-going secularists. Best of all, they'll have been with you in church all that time. You can say that they were raised in a *Christian home*, and their irreligious ways are their own fault.

Appendix C

The God of Fun

One value which we seem to seek to shape in our children is the value of fun. Fun is an unquestioned, undisputed right of children.

Fun, fun, fun. Learning at school must be fun, and curricula are now judged on how much fun they make the learning process. School holidays must be fun, and a veritable industry of holiday activities and entertainments now exists. Sports must be fun, and it is the supposed inherent fun of beating others at games that I suppose makes sports so central to our culture. Eating breakfast must have fun pictures on the box, fun toys inside and fun sugary food to boot. Observe the mountain of toys in the average Western child's bedroom. What he or she needs most is fun, and Mom and Dad will buy it. Brushing our teeth must be done with fun-shaped toothbrushes, and fun-tasting toothpaste. Bathing must include toys, so that fun may be had in the act of cleaning oneself. Pyjamas must have fun pictures on them, and so must the blankets. And at the top of this fun-list is television. Television producers have been masters at creating and satisfying the appetite for fun. Immediate, interesting, amusing, startling, comical, and ever-changing moving images keep the fun-levels high. And a child without a steady diet of TV has no fun, you see.

Perhaps I am not exaggerating when I say that our culture regards fun as the greatest good when it comes to children. Fun is the supreme goal for children. I am not sure at what point this supreme value loses its centrality, but at some point, the bored young humans are introduced to the truth, "Life's not all about fun, you know!" This cynical statement is a rather heartless and violent introduction to reality, since nothing in all the child's existence could have revealed this fact. From the rising of the sun to the going down of the same, the child is to have fun.

I don't know all the origins of this fun-as-supreme-value ethic. I suspect much of it began with Romanticism's idealising of the child as the paragon of innocence and virtue, and therefore thinking it deserving of a childhood of uncomplicated play. However, as a parent and pastor, I am concerned with how this idea will shape the religious imagination of my children, and the children in my congregation. I'm worried about how teaching our children to love fun above all else will become a major stumbling-block to their worship. Because the fun-ethic has not escaped church life.

Observe what we ask our children when they come out of Sunday School. "Did you have fun?" Indeed, that's what we expect from our children's programmes: fun. The materials must be colourful and fun to look at. The activities must be interesting and fun to do. Fun games need to be played. The songs must be full of movement, comical gestures and catchy tunes. They must be fun to sing. The lessons must be funny, zany and fun to listen to. And we judge them a success if our children return with the ultimate value statement: "That was fun!" When someone has a talent for fun-making, we remark, "He's really good with the children!" Yes, if a child thinks church is fun, they will like it. And hopefully, we reason, they'll become Christians.

The problem is this: at what point, and in what way, do we graduate our children to the understanding that God is not fun? The fear of the Lord is not a "fun" experience. Singing "Holy, Holy, Holy" is not fun. One thinks of words like sobriety, awe, hope, or adoration to describe the experience, but fun is not one of them. Preparing sermons is not fun. I enjoy doing it, and am greatly enriched by the intense study of God's Word. But it isn't fun, like Tetris, or playing fetch with my dog. Nor is listening to a patient explanation of God's Word. Illuminating, encouraging, challenging, provocative, perhaps, but not fun. Prayer is not fun. Intense concentration, focus and meditation on God's revealed character is penetrating, revealing, satisfying, exhilarating and exhausting. But it is not fun. And the Lord's Supper is never fun. Daunting, intimidating, heart-rending, welcoming, refreshing, but never fun. Worship is not fun, and yet we think fun is the key to creating little worshippers.

Why does fun remain so central to church ministry?

First, our culture simply takes it for granted. It is the way we do things. Therefore, to question it is to disturb the way the machine runs.

Second, pragmatism guides our methods. We want our children to be in church, and to worship, so we figure that fun ought to be brought in to hook them on church. This is not different from using rock and pop music, promising your best life now, or offering a car raffle in the foyer of the church. We think that ends justify means.

Third, we create and sustain this appetite in so many ways outside of church. I grew up in the fun culture, and pass it on without thinking. But what did children do before the world smothered them with its overflowing, laughing box of fun in the last two centuries? They found things to do and make. They learned things. They helped at home. Where they could, they read. They played music with their families. They worshipped at church. And they played. In other words, they were little humans preparing for their adult lives.

We are always shaping our children's affections, by what we love, and what we expect from them. If we expect them to not only play, but work and serve, they learn that fun is not central to life. If we insist that they must learn, even when that learning is not fun, we teach them what learning is like in real life. If we send them outdoors to amuse themselves with sticks and rocks and mud and dead birds, like children always have, we shape them to find and create enjoyment, not wait for it to be given to them. And more to the heart of the matter of the affections: if we teach them to be motivated by the truth, goodness and beauty of things and actions, we teach them to value things for what they are, not merely for what they supply. If we remove fun as the governing arbiter of value, we prepare them to love things for what they are worth, not merely for what kind of ephemeral thrill they provide. If we insist that they learn to live with their immature boredom with worship, we teach them to postpone their judgement on what they do not yet understand. In other words, we prepare them to be worshippers, not consumers.

And perhaps we will see them still worshipping in twenty years.

About the author:

David de Bruyn and his wife have three children and live in Johannesburg, South Africa, where he has pastored and taught on Christian radio for over fourteen years. He blogs at conservativechristianity.wordpress.com.

47061359R00059

Made in the USA
Lexington, KY
03 August 2019